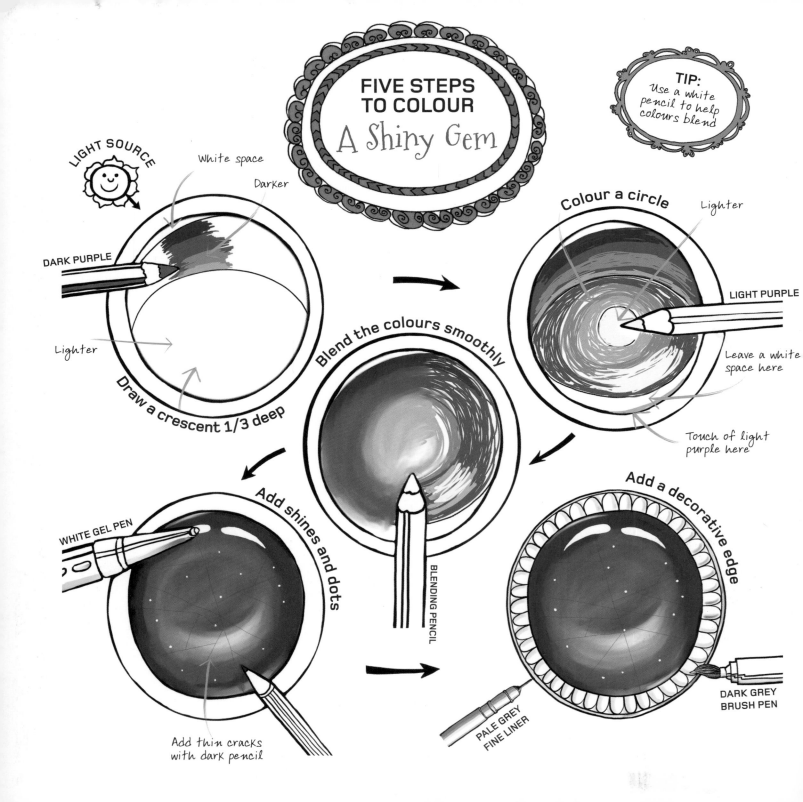

Tangle Magic

A SPELLBINDING COLOURING BOOK
WITH HIDDEN CHARMS

Jessica Palmer

Dedication

For Granny Madge who gave me childhood magic.

For Becky Raine, my wise guide.

And for Cherie, Heather, Claire and Lucy, and colouring stars worldwide.

First published in 2016

Search Press Limited, Wellwood, North Farm Road,
Tunbridge Wells, Kent, TN2 3DR

Text and illustration copyright © Jessica Palmer, 2016

Design copyright © Search Press, 2016

ISBN: 978-1-78221-463-2

Printed in China

This book belongs to:

....

You are invited to join FanTangle Coloring Friends
on Facebook. It's a friendly place where you can
post your work, share tips and ideas and the
pleasure of colouring Tangle Wood, Tangle Bay
and Tangle Magic.

Please also like and share the
Tangle Wood Colouring Book page.

Why not also set up a colouring club? Get together
with friends and share pens, pencils and all the
fun of colouring.

Welcome to Tangle Magic

Welcome to the wonderful world of Tangle Magic – a place of enchantment
filled with dragons, fairy tale characters and mythical creatures. Enter this
place of fascination and intrigue, and let your imagination meander through
a mystical land of legends, wizardry and bewitchment. Draw, doodle and
dream, and cast a colourful spell on every page.

These are some of the hidden charms scattered
in Tangle Magic:

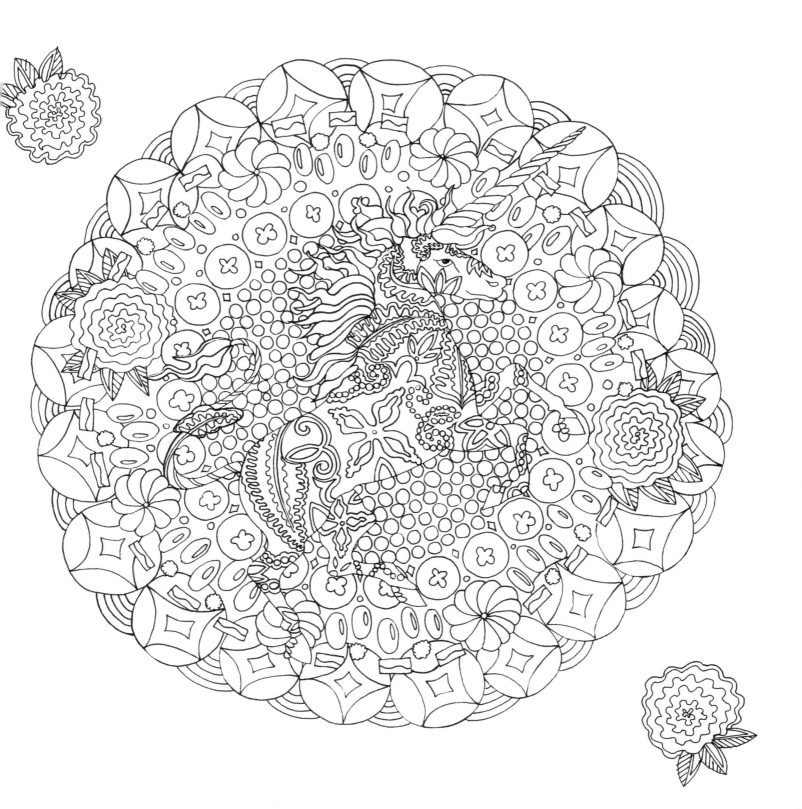

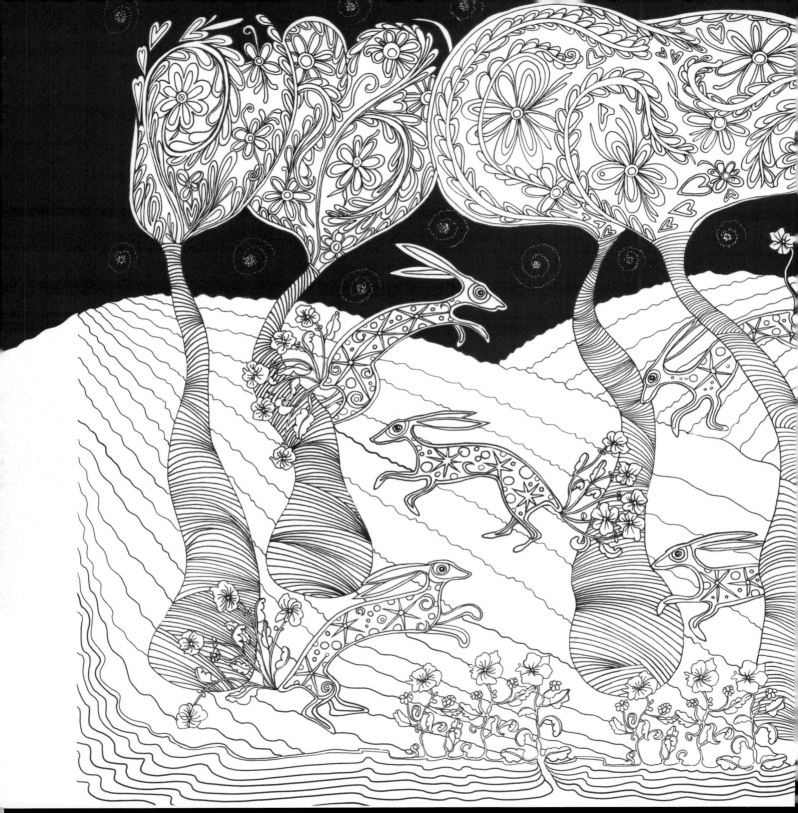

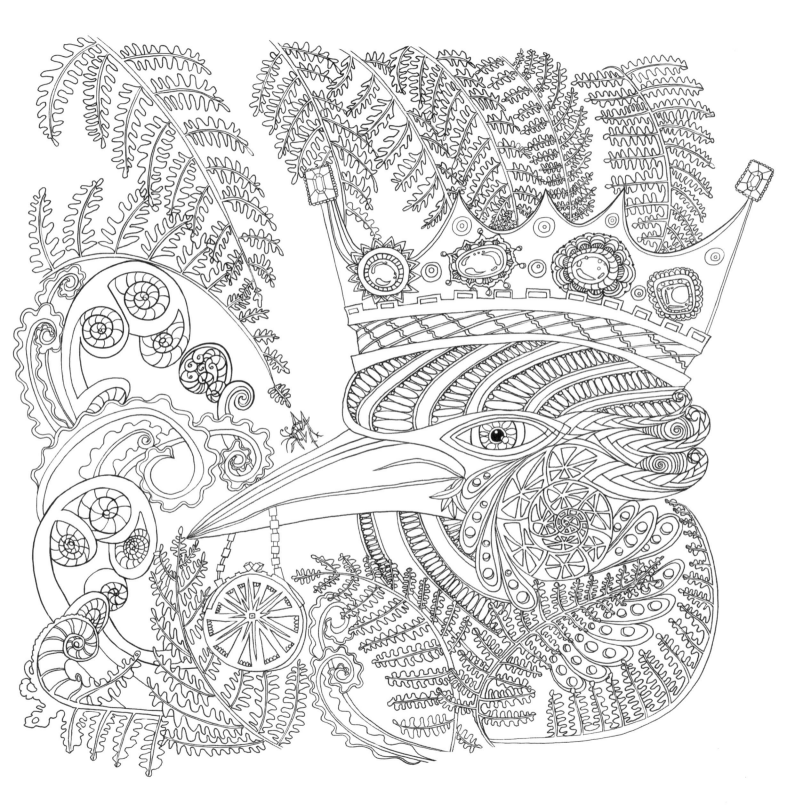

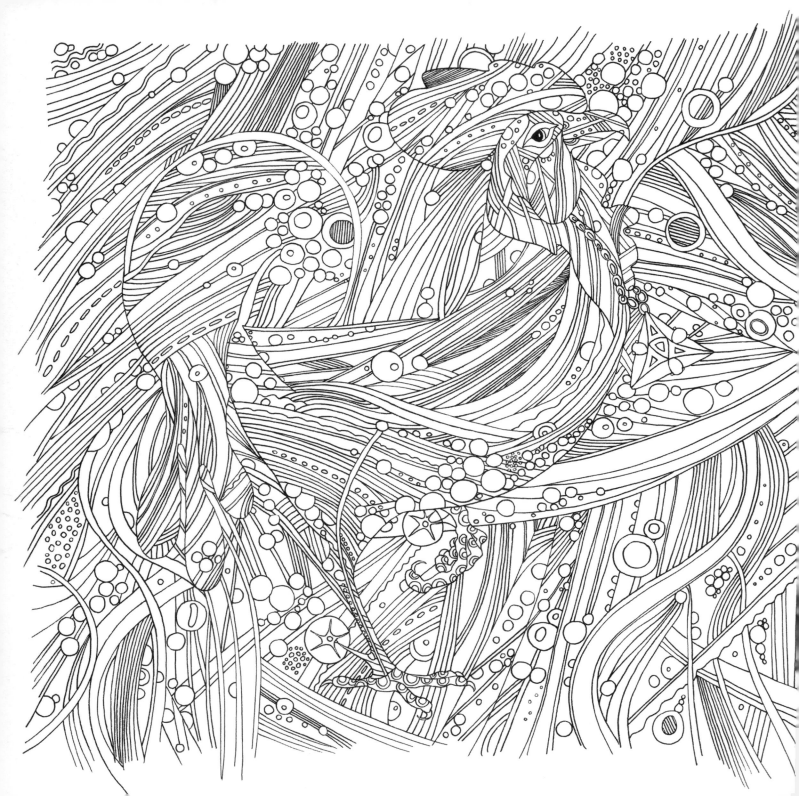

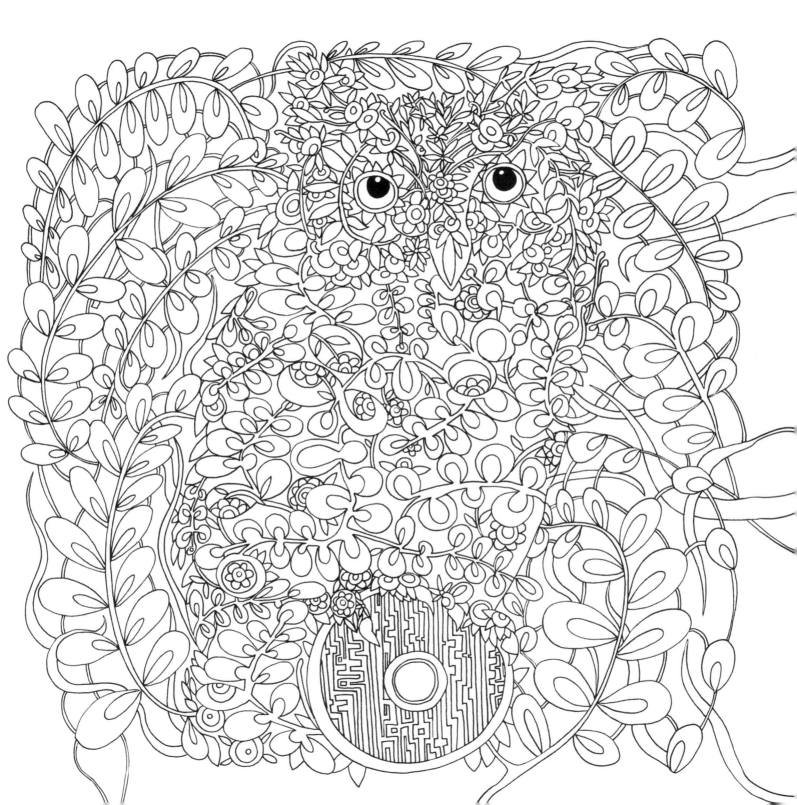

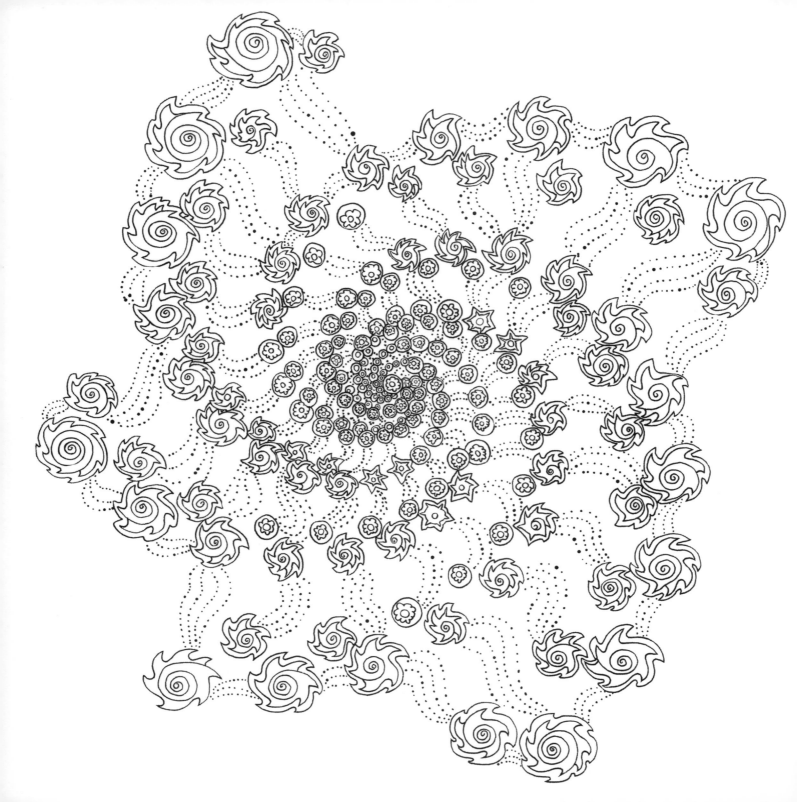

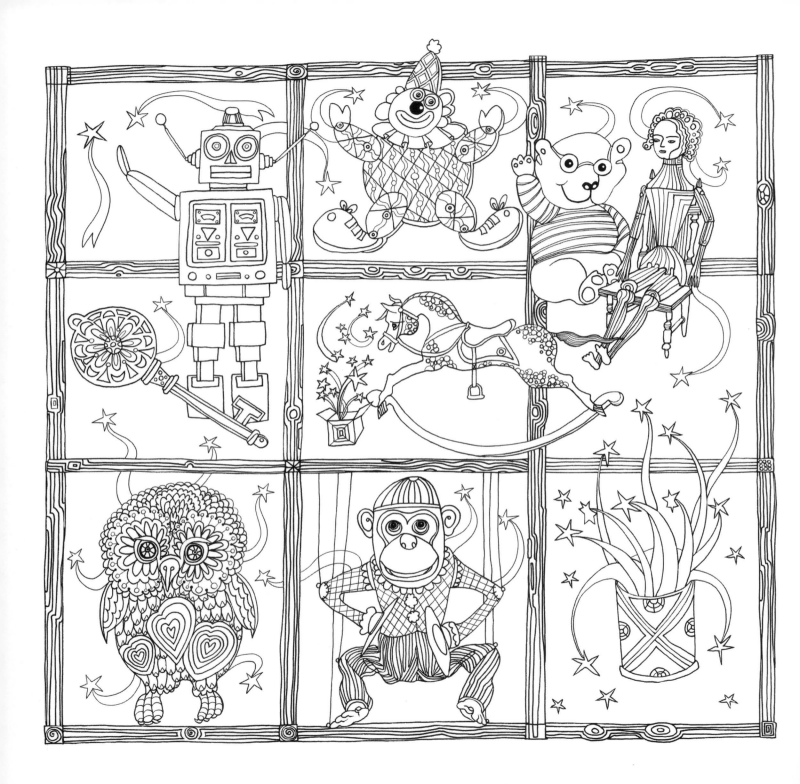